FRANK LLOYD WRIGHT'S
INTERIORS

FRANK LLOYD WRIGHT'S
INTERIORS

Thomas A. Heinz

Gramercy Books
New York

This 2002 edition is published by
Gramercy Books™, an imprint of
Random House Value Publishing, Inc.,
280 Park Avenue, New York, NY 10017

Gramercy Books™ and design are
trademarks of Random House Value
Publishing, Inc.

Random House
New York • Toronto • London
Sydney • Auckland

http://www.randomhouse.com/

Printed in Italy

ISBN 0-517-21969-7

10 9 8 7 6 5 4 3 2 1

*Dedicated to Wes Peters, a wise and
knowledgeable associate of Frank Lloyd
Wright who was perhaps the most
enthusiastic of all the apprentices.*

It is essential that a workable system
of preservation and restoration be
coordinated between the existing
owners of the many remaining
examples of Frank Lloyd Wright's
buildings for, unless they are
maintained in their original colours,
materials and arrangements, how can
anyone make a proper assessment of
their worth, even to the point of
whether they like them or not. An
assessment cannot be made based on
photographs, or on memories of
buildings that no longer reflect the
work as Wright conceived and
approved it and personally directed its
execution. Wright's work is too
important to allow further deterioration
and demolition and readers must try to
participate in this effort of preservation,
even if it is only to involve others in
the appreciation of Wright's work.

For as long as Wright had been designing buildings, he had given as much care and attention to their interiors, regarding them as the spaces defined by the structures he had created.

In the beginning, Wright's interiors were not untypical of others of the period. But once he began to experiment, other original and startling options began to present themselves.

Wright utilized materials in unusual ways; for example, he used brick instead of the usual ceramic tiles in his fireplaces. He brought to the inside materials more commonly seen on the outside, adding an unusual cohesion to the whole design. He had a true understanding of the nature of materials, their innate beauty, and their usefulness. He preferred wood, such as quarter-sawn oak, in its natural state, where its quality could shine through. He liked natural flaws, seeing a strange beauty in irregularity and realizing that nature rarely achieves perfection, but bestows character and individuality instead.

While his preference was for

JAMES CHARNLEY HOUSE, CHICAGO, ILLINOIS, 1891

Louis Sullivan, Wright's employer at the time, was not known for innovative lighting and the lobby (right) shows the hand of Wright, who used various skylights, clerestories and windows in unusual locations. Wright often eliminated diagonals caused by items such as stairways which, in this case, is concealed behind the wall to the right. This design clearly illustrates several techniques used by Wright in later projects that were not features of Sullivan's work.

GEORGE BLOSSOM HOUSE, CHICAGO, ILLINOIS, 1892 DINING ROOM (RIGHT)
Wright based his designs on the proportions of the human frame, rather as Leonardo da Vinci depicted in his drawing of more than 500 years ago and which shows a man inscribed within a circle and a square. Wright, at 5ft 8in (1.7m), with his arms raised and fully extended, would have been able to perfectly describe the arch separating the living and dining rooms of the Blossom House.

The arch perfectly complements the rounded window bay of the dining room, with its art-glass reminiscent of windows in paintings by Dutch Masters hundreds of years earlier.

This is a most sophisticated design for a 25-year-old with only six years of experience in his field.

There was also built-in furniture, which Wright specially designed for the room.

8

WILLIAM H. WINSLOW HOUSE, RIVER FOREST, ILLINOIS, 1893

OLD DINING BAY

Wright's interiors are complex, with the space often organized differently within a single room. The wooden half-walls separate the space containing the round bay, with its continuous window seat, from the more formal area containing the dining table. The ceiling of the bay is also lower than that of the other part of the room. The bay was often used for afternoon tea and shows a small table covered with a cloth.

WILLIAM H. WINSLOW HOUSE, RIVER FOREST, ILLINOIS, 1893

ENTRY

This is one of Wright's few houses that had an outside front door leading directly into the house, the door being to the left of this photograph.

The entry is as spatially complex as any in the Winslow House. It leads to the living room, which is directly opposite the library, shown here. The arched door with the art-glass panel leads to the second-floor staircase, while another leads to the dining room.

By the newel posts, the floor level is raised and there is a fireplace opposite the front door which is set behind a screen of posts and arches smaller than those of the doors.

The glass patterns in the Winslow House derive from two sources, that in the entry hall and the second-floor windows seemingly metamorphosed from two Egyptian designs found in a German pattern book once owned by Wright.

The mural was painted long after the Winslows had moved out.

natural forms, his forte was to take American vernacular architecture and apply the benefits of modern technology to it.

This was an important step in Wight's personal revolution. His houses were conceived as complete experiences, so it was all the more startling for clients when they were called upon to abandon the trappings of their former lives when taking possession of their new Wright house.

Wright considered the needs and requirements of his clients and would literally tailor a design

FRANK LLOYD WRIGHT HOUSE, OAK PARK, ILLINOIS, 1895

PLAYROOM BAY WINDOW (CENTRE)
The pattern of the glass in these windows is very similar to that used elsewhere in Oak Park, in the Unity Temple of 1906, and is not the original. It replaces that which was broken by one or more of Wright's six children. While the glass pattern is composed of vertical lines, when all the panels are lined up, the effect is of a strong horizontal which conforms to the wood trim used throughout the room.

PLAYROOM (TOP RIGHT)
The inspiration for this room may have been the ballroom of the

Auditorium Building that Wright had worked on while at the Adler & Sullivan architectural practice in Chicago. It too had a barrel vault with wooden trim alternating down the barrel and central skylight. What it did not have were bays on each of the longitudinal sides that extended the space horizontally, interrupting the plain brick walls.

LIVING ROOM (BELOW FAR RIGHT)
The living room is filled with furniture originally designed for the Robie House. The walls and trim are as near to the original as possible; the thin wooden strip at the top of the room openings, called the headline, disengages the walls

below it, making them appear as if they were shoji screens used in traditional Japanese houses. The fireplace is to the extreme left and located within an inglenook off the main area of the living room.

accordingly. Peter Beachy was a tall man, so his house was designed to suit him physically. Conversely, the Smiths of Bloomfield Hills were short and their house mirrored this fact.

Wright was willing to design anything that a client requested and what they did not ask for he would sell to them, which not only increased his fee but also made for a harmonious design.

Did Wright design for specific interiors or specific locations, or was there a degree of interchangeability? The latter is more likely to be the case. However, scale, colour, texture and ambience were important considerations. If he could not find the appropriate piece of furniture, he would design it himself, so important was it that it should be in harmony with the space it occupied. This is the typical response of the architect.

Wright was fiercely individualistic and established certain principles and standards that he adhered to for most of his career. Even so, he was never

B. Harley Bradley House, Kankakee, Illinois, 1900

LIVING ROOM

Wright had used built-in furniture from his earliest days, and once he began to produce his own original designs this practice continued. The wooden strips on the ceiling are remedial, though the ceilings are generally flat throughout the building.

static, and was constantly re-inventing his style. One of his preoccupations was an emphasis on the horizontal. This is reflected in his use of a special size of Roman brick that is longer as well as thinner than the standard one.

To add to the beauty of a design, he often used a golden-brown brick, known as iron-spot, which was made from Ohio clay that contained iron. When it was fired, the specks of iron turned dark, almost black, and became slightly iridescent. It was used on the Robie House and other Prairie houses which, for the most part, had low pitched roofs and overhanging eaves in the style of the early Midwest. The same wood colour and finish were used on both interior and exterior.

Windows were flush to walls; some were inset, while others protruded to the outside of the building. Stained-glass windows, which Wright referred to as lightscreens, were used where large areas of plate glass were usually to be seen. Wright used metal cames to divide glass, creating stylized patterns in a highly decorative manner.

Wright's preoccupation with the horizontal took the form of a continuous headline which connected the tops of the windows and doors. This was set at 6ft 8in (2m), the height of a standard residential door. (Doors were once taller or shorter, but once building codes came into being, the standard, rather than the requirements of the architect, became the norm.) Wright

used this device over and over again to produce interiors that bear his unmistakable trademark.

The single most important element in Wright's buildings is light, which is not to say that there are no dark areas. It is the contrast, the placement, and the quality of that light that defines and moulds the spaces that makes Wright's approach so unique. Regardless of the size or the cost of the building, his mastery of lighting is always in evidence.

Are these interiors unique, or are they mere curiosities? Are they based on firm principles that makes them work and that set precedents for future architecture? Wright did

WARD W. WILLITTS HOUSE, HIGHLAND PARK, ILLINOIS, 1901

LIVING ROOM (OPPOSITE BELOW)

This house has been described as a masterpiece among the Prairie houses, which were largely conceived as being horizontal in form, often of one storey, and with rooms flowing one into another in a continuous space.

The living room is large at about 24 x 27ft (7 x 8m), in fact similar in size to the Coonley House of nearly ten years later. The shelved niches at the corners and the built-in furniture along the side walls allow for as much floor space as possible.

THE OLD LIVING ROOM (RIGHT)

THE OLD BEDROOM (BELOW)

ARTHUR HEURTLEY HOUSE, OAK PARK, ILLINOIS, 1902

DINING/LIVING ROOM

The structure of the ceilings of this house is not reflected on the exterior, which has a simple hipped roof. The long gable of the dining room is trimmed with multi-section ceiling boards that are set to coincide with the structure that supports them. In the living room, the hipped pattern presents a very forward-looking design which was later used in the first Taliesin and again in Aline Barnsdall's Hollyhock House.

GEORGE BARTON HOUSE, BUFFALO, NEW YORK, 1903

LIVING ROOM

Wright put a great deal of work and effort into this interior, as it had been commissioned by Darwin D. Martin for his brother-in-law, George, to see what Wright could do before commissioning a house for himself. Martin was an executive of the Larkin company, that once rivalled Sears Roebuck and Montgomery Ward, and his approval meant a great deal to Wright as a source of potential commissions.

SUSAN LAWRENCE DANA HOUSE, SPRINGFIELD, ILLINOIS, 1903

There are many spectacular interiors in the Dana House, the dining room being one of three multi-level spaces. The other two are the front entry, with its sculpture entitled 'Flower in the Crannied Wall' (left), which is a three-storey space, and the studio which may also be considered to be three storeys high.

In the dining room with its entry fountain (BELOW), the electric lighting may be one of the most interesting features. Most of it is indirect, set behind the two long sides of the sumac and birch tree mural, while at the bottom of the lighting trough is a beautiful set of art-glass laylights.

In each of the four corners are pendent lights referred to as butterfly lights, though the connection with butterflies seems tenuous. They are complex three-dimension arrangements whose flat panels have some deceiving angles.

There is much original furniture, the largest group in any single building of the Prairie era. The tall-backed chairs create a smaller, more intimate space for dining around the table, and the stylized natural forms surrounding it make a meal more like a picnic.

SUSAN LAWRENCE DANA HOUSE, SPRINGFIELD, ILLINOIS, 1903

MASTER BEDROOM

There are no known photographs of the original placement of the furniture designed and built especially for the master bedroom of the Dana House. Moreover, there are no drawings that would indicate the intended or ideal placement of these pieces. Unlike most other Prairie houses, there are few built-in pieces of furniture, and nearly all are free-standing.

The heavy trim of the cathedral ceiling occurs with the same regularity as the wooden roof rafters that hold it in place.

On the right of the photograph is a drapery rod that once held heavy velvet curtains that blocked-off the bed area and may have been used to conserve the heat from the fireplace between the beds.

DARWIN D. MARTIN HOUSE, BUFFALO, NEW YORK, 1904

DINING ROOM (LEFT BELOW)

The original interior would have been considerably softened by a lime-green thick-pile rug under the custom furniture. The dining room is defined by walls on three sides and a deck at the headline on the fourth side.

NEW LIVING ROOM (BELOW)

The room is similar in concept to the living room of the Barton House which was built before Darwin Martin's and was situated next to it.

Not all of the original furnishings have made it to the 21st century.

not throw groups of disparate elements together and hope for the best; there was a serious intention that needs to be understood so that future generations can benefit from his genius.

As to the overall design, there is much debate as to where the interior starts and the exterior ends. Broad roofs extend far beyond most of the walls that support them. The walls may be serpentine, zig-zagging back and forth from deep inside out to the fascia edge of the roof and occasionally beyond. One can be under the roof with various parts of the building in front and to both sides, and yet still be not actually inside.

In Wright's later designs of his Usonian period, when flat roofs were introduced, more economy was practised, and the distinction between outside and in became generally more blurred. Long rows of paired doors were introduced that made the walls seem to disappear.

Concrete floor slabs used on the interior continued, seemingly in an unbroken line, out onto the patio. Even the scored block patterns, or unit lines, as Wright described them, continued the illusion of space extending beyond the walls: to further confuse the eye, furniture and planters were set outside which mirrored those of the interior.

While the exact size and scale

MARY ADAMS HOUSE, HIGHLAND PARK, ILLINOIS, 1905

ENTRY HALL (OPPOSITE)

Just inside the entrance of this house is a space which is typical of Wright's more modest houses. The trim has substantially darkened, however, as a result of the passage of time and the effects of light over the previous 90 or so years.

During the period before the work of wholesale restoration began, walls in many of Wright's houses were covered in a natural-looking grass cloth. This was not painted but its colour was fixed into the material in much the same way that Wright mixed colour into the interior plaster. Moreover, the

wooden trim that is a feature of nearly all of the Prairie houses is also here, while baseboards that are typical of all houses are taller in this house.

Bases are composed of three parts: a shoe between the floor material, usually 2¼-in (6-cm) wide oak strip flooring, and the baseboard, which is usually of oak and about 6-in wide (15-cm) and extends around the base of all the walls. On the top of the baseboard is a trim that frames the wall plaster. The corners are protected by the trim that is mitred at the plaster corners. This trim is normally 2¼-in wide.

This dimension appears many

times in Wright's designs, from this period through to the end of his long career. The upper horizontal trim defining each room is often called the headline and is located at the top of the doors and windows, usually at the 6ft 8-in (2-m) level, the height of a standard door.

At the left of centre is a framed vertical section that delineates a post or column. In Wright houses, the structural system is expressed by these and other similar protuberances in the walls and ceilings. While these elements express it, they are not the actual structure. Wright's interiors are too sophisticated for such brutal details.

of the interiors were determined by Wright, they were initially dictated by the needs and suggestions of the clients. These were discerning people and for the most part knew what they wanted, though they could be influenced by Wright, who not only met their expectations but usually exceeded them.

There were times in Wright's 70-year-long career that it became difficult to define a typical Wright interior. It was not to be found in the Robie, Martin or Dana houses of the Prairie era, nor in Aline Barnsdall's Hollyhock House, with its dark and cavernous spaces. Fallingwater is also atypical with its restrained use of wood and flamboyant cantilevers.

Perhaps it is not to these American palaces that one should look, but to more modest examples, perhaps back to the beginning of the Prairie period and the Hunt House of LaGrange, Chicago, which contains more of the typical elements to be found in the majority of the houses, such as the strong horizontal headline. This links the windows with the doors; the wall above this line is the same colour as the ceiling and could be considered a part of the ceiling.

The headline gives bold definition to each room. It runs flush to the wall on the west side of the living room, defining the cantilever thickness of the deck that separates the living and dining rooms. The grouped, or ribbon windows (occasionally alternating with a door of the same width and detail as the windows), are to be found on three of the four sides of the first floor, as well as on the second.

The tall, three-part baseboard follows the bottom of walls. There are flat boards alongside each window and door as well as on each outside corner, spanning the distance between the baseboard at the bottom and the headline at the

WILLIAM R. HEATH HOUSE, BUFFALO, NEW YORK, 1905

ENTRY

The wood detailing used in the Heath House is typical of the best of the Prairie houses. The horizontal headband defines where the wall ends and the point at which the colour of the ceiling begins. All of the plaster panels are square or rectangular and are defined by horizontal and vertical trim, the same trim that is located at each corner. The floor defines the lower horizontal plane and the stairs that are placed below it are followed along the wall and baseboard by 1-in (2.5-cm) trim aligned with the edge of each tread.

To the right is a small but separate reception room, common at the time in houses of this quality. The small opening to the left of the door chimes leads to the stairway which rises up to the second floor. The next door opening leads down the hall to the kitchen and servants' rooms.

The dining room can just be seen between the last two piers. There was a full set of custom furniture designed by Wright. It was refinished in a light colour, but was removed many years ago.

top. The jamb casings stop at the headline well before they reach the ceiling, which leaves the ceiling as well as the upper wall free of vertical trim.

The ceiling treatment of the Hunt House is subtle in that the line of the wood trim follows along the wall and abuts 2ft (.6m) from it; but unlike the headline, it passes over the deck between the living and dining rooms and extends into the dining room, as does the space below the deck.

This was intentional on Wright's part. Blurring the line between wall and ceiling makes the location of the ceiling ambiguous and since it is generally above the line of sight, makes it seem higher than its actual dimensions.

UNITY TEMPLE, OAK PARK, ILLINOIS, 1906

The traditional stone church across the street from Unity Temple, with its tower and rose window, was a great deal more costly to build than Unity Temple, though they both seat about the same number of people. Wright's design is also more compact and could nearly fit into the area to the side of the church.

The interior is a complex matrix of three-dimensional spaces. The flush panels next to the pulpit are the doors that open into the lobby and entry, the direction that parishioners would take after the service.

TEMPLE ROOM (BELOW)

MEETING ROOM (OPPOSITE)

The four-square plan was developed while Walter Burley Griffin was working in the Wright office. Griffin used it almost exclusively on all his houses, adding porches, extending rooms and cleverly developing many alternative exterior schemes. Wright used this same plan over many years, when it came to be regarded as a model for the Prairie house. It was published in the *Ladies' Home Journal* of April 1907, used in the

Hunt House that same year, and continued through to 1916.

The front half of the square is the living room; half of the remaining space at the back is the dining room with no wall separating it from the living room, while the other half is the kitchen with partitions between the living and the dining rooms. A stairway up to the main living area and which continues up to the second floor is inserted between the

living room and the kitchen.

A house of this design was usually built with dimensions of about 900sq ft (84m²) per floor. The second floor would be divided into three or four bedrooms and a small bathroom. Including the entry on the outside, the total volume for the entire building would approach 2,000sq ft (186m²). The dimensions are to a certain extent based on the greatest length that a 2 x 12-ft floor board can span without cutting it.

UNITY TEMPLE, OAK PARK, ILLINOIS, 1906

The main temple or auditorium space can be described as a large cube. However, it is that and much more – in fact it is one of the most complex of the major spaces of Wright's Prairie era. The other would be the now-lost Larkin Building. Overall, the room does not feel dark and all of the light sources are from high up in the space. The skylight at the centre and the clerestory windows on all four sides are all set deeply into their frames, preventing direct light from entering, which is reflected off various surfaces and is well diffused throughout the area. The clerestories form continuous lines of windows between the columns. These open as pivoted screens along its length and have no defining frames.

ROOKERY BUILDING, CHICAGO, ILLINOIS, 1905 (RIGHT AND OPPOSITE)
Recently restored, the sparkling lobby is surrounded on all four sides by the 11-storey building. The floor of the balcony is of glass bricks which were manufactured by the Luxfer Prism Company, partly owned by the building's proprietor, Edward C. Waller.

The gold leaf is visible on the upper section of the spandrels of the stairs. Also visible is the florid design that was executed by Wright and which is not his usual style. However, the flower urns sitting on the top of the lower newel posts are very similar to those which he designed for houses of the Prairie era.

When the term 'form follows function' is applied to Wright's architecture, it means that the exterior reflects but does not reproduce what is on the exterior, even though there is a correlation between the two. Wright maintained that it was the space within that was defined by his walls, ceilings and floors, rather than vice versa. He demonstrated his theory by using a cup and indicating the space enclosed by it.

Although many of the images of Wright's buildings are concentrated on exterior views and elevations, mainly because his work was mostly residential and thus not open to public view, he regarded the interiors as the more important, as enclosed spaces where his clients lived their lives. Of course, nowadays, more and more of Wright's houses are becoming accessible to visitors, or are

becoming family foundations dedicated to their preservation.

Wright's primary aim was to satisfy the needs of his clients. Buildings were intended to accommodate the activities that they would perform within them and, since they were machines for living, it was Wright's intention to produce something that was beautiful and which worked.

The way in which Wright

manipulated natural light seems to have varied throughout his career and the four periods into which it can be divided. The interiors of his early period, 1886–1900, were brighter than those of other houses of the Victorian era. His windows tended to be larger than normal, which was a result of changes of proportion and the sizes of the rooms enclosed.

During the Prairie era,

1900–1910, Wright's houses appeared darker because the rooms were larger and deeper and dark corners were created within. Moreover, deep roof overhangs, large roof cantilevers, and deep-set windows also had the effect of reducing natural light.

From about 1910–1932, when Wright's personal life was in chaos, windows seemed to reduce in size and were set even deeper into the

FERDINAND F. TOMEK HOUSE, RIVERSIDE, ILLINOIS, 1907

DINING ROOM

There is much discussion concerning the similarities between the earlier Tomek House and the Robie House. This is more true of the exterior than the interior. The continuous line of windows along the wall to the right and the lowered ceiling at the outboard edges of the living and dining rooms is also quite similar. There may be the same type of long steel supports along the longitudinal changes in ceiling heights. However, there are no ceiling lights at the Robie House.

Wright did explore the extension of space over and through

the mass at the central fireplace and stairwell. A mirror is utilized above the built-in sideboard to reflect the dining room ceiling, whereas in the Robie House the

space actually pierces this mass.

Tomek was in the lumber business and this may be the reason for the oak-strip floors with their herringbone pattern.

ISABEL ROBERTS HOUSE, RIVER FOREST, ILLINOIS, 1908

The Native American rugs used in this modest interior are much simpler than one might expect in an original Wright interior. The custom furniture used here is made of fir, the same wood that was used on the trim throughout the house.

The room features several adjustable chairs which feature in other Wright houses.

Isabel Roberts, an architect herself, worked in Wright's office during the Prairie years.

AVERY COONLEY HOUSE, RIVERSIDE, ILLINOIS, 1908 LIVING ROOM (OPPOSITE)
The Coonley commission was for a large house and Coonley himself was avant-garde enough for Wright to fully explore structural and spatial possibilities. The wood trim details were as developed as the Heath House, but the cathedral ceiling and its trim, with integral lighting, surpasses nearly everything that came before.

Wright designed in the negative space on the ceiling pattern. In the first Taliesin, as well as in the Hollyhock House, Wright installed

trim and painted panels along the creases and edges of the ceiling planes. Here at the Coonley House, these areas are left blank with the fields of each ceiling plane filled with trim. The edges are defined by a very wide board of quarter-sawn oak. The pitch of each plane is identified with the vertical boards.

A broad band of highly detailed grilles fills the bottom of each plane. Behind these grilles are two sets of incandescent lights, switched separately, that provide a beautiful, soft light similar to that used in the Robie House.

The fireplace is one of the most refined but also one of the most simple of the Prairie era. The fireplace breast, above the firebox, is set forward of the stud wall while the firebox is defined at the bottom by large limestone blocks. The blocks also define the top of the built-in seating outboard of the fireplace. The blank plaster panels above the book shelves on each side of the fireplace were once covered with silk, painted with scenes of delicate birch trees and soft green ferns. Sadly, they have long since been removed.

EDWARD E. BOYNTON HOUSE, ROCHESTER, NEW YORK, 1908

DINING ROOM

This is one of the largest and most elaborate of the Wright-designed dining rooms for which there are two full sets of tables and chairs.

The table is illuminated by two sources, by light-posts and by an overhead panel. The four light-posts, two at each end of the table, are attached to the leaves of the table-top.

The ends of the table pull out to accommodate several leaves that allows the table to extend to nearly the entire length of the room. The light-posts travel with the end leaves which are held off the floor by spiral castors that roll with the extensions. Only the Dana House has such a flamboyantly complex arrangement.

The table has eight legs, four for the centre panel, that is placed above the electrical outlet for the light-posts, and two each for the extendable leaves.

The three ceiling light panels above the table replace what would normally be a chandelier hung from the centre of the dining room ceiling and would have only illuminated a limited area. Wright wanted a more flexible arrangement so that the light could be more evenly dispersed along the length of the table.

The most dramatic element of the dining room is the enormous breakfront cabinet behind the dining room table. It is one of Wright's largest and certainly most impressive.

FREDERICK C. ROBIE HOUSE, CHICAGO, ILLINOIS, 1909

LIVING ROOM

It is unfortunate that the original furniture is in a nearby museum and not in the house for which it was designed. The cantilevered couch and the two small stools or tables are original to the room, but the upholstered chairs were introduced when the house was a conference centre. If one compares this with the Tomek House (page 36), the refinement that occurred in the few years between the commissions becomes immediately apparent.

TALIESIN I, SPRING GREEN, WISCONSIN, 1911 DINING ROOM AND BEDROOMS

These rooms at the first Taliesin are given a sense of cohesion by means of the oatmeal-coloured fabrics embroidered with circular patterns in shades of green, blue, yellow and vermilion, and are as intense as the colours of the Japanese screens installed on the walls behind the dining room furniture and the large double bed. The incorporation of Japanese art continued throughout the many fires, rebuilding and alterations that Taliesin was subjected to throughout the last 90 years.

The dining room is where Mamah Borthwick Cheney, her children and some apprentices, sat enjoying their lunch on an August day in 1914, before they were brutally murdered and a large part of the complex burned down.

FRANCIS W. LITTLE HOUSE (NORTHOME) WAYZATA, MINNESOTA 1913 LIVING ROOM

For some reason, the cantilevered couch from the original Robie House has found its way into this room, but it does seem to harmonize with other furniture originally designed for the Littles' previous Peoria house of 1903, as well as the new designs for this much larger house, the largest of Wright's early career.

The house was later dismantled in the 1980s and rebuilt inside the Metropolitan Museum of Art in New York as a permanent exhibit. All of the furniture, wood trim and flooring are original. Only the two track lights installed on the upper soffits are new to the room. Wright himself specified the light-coloured , unpatterned rug as suitable for this room.

MIDWAY GARDENS, CHICAGO, ILLINOIS, 1914 WINTER GARDEN (BELOW)
This large interior space has many similarities to the temple room of Oak Park's Unity Temple of eight years earlier. This also had two balconies, joined at the corners by concealed stair towers.

Lighting similar to that in the living rooms of the Coonley and Robie Houses, consisting of incandescent bulbs behind intricate grilles, was also incorporated here, but it is quite unlike the plain hanging lights used in the corners of Unity Temple; here they are much more playful, with large beads and pyramids forming part of the chains that suspend them from the ceiling. Custom furniture was designed for this room but was never built.

walls. In California, in particular, windows were small, almost as if Wright were actively preventing the sun from entering the house.

The Usonian period, from 1932–1959, began a dramatic reversal and houses were thrown open to the light, although direct sunlight was restricted and carefully controlled. Usonian houses had banks of clear, plate-glass doors, taller than usual, and many of them had transoms above. Areas of darkness were also a feature of Usonian houses, but rows of clerestory windows directed light deep into the interiors, creating areas of sharp relief.

The spatial variety that Wright was able to bring to his interiors is much greater than that of other architects, which may have been

FREDERICK C. BOGK HOUSE, MILWAUKEE, WISCONSIN, 1916

DINING ROOM

This fine dining room was designed in the spirit of the Prairie era, with headline trim uniting doors and windows and wide boards on the high ceiling.

The built-in sideboard incorporates two unusual features not often found in Wright's work. These are the lights on the sides of the base cabinet, which have small shades that are in keeping with the overall Oriental feeling of the whole house. To the back of the cabinet is a piece of original Japanese art that is illuminated by the two lights.

The carpet is the original Wright design and was made up by the Milwaukee firm of Niedecken-Wallbridge, a company that often collaborated with Wright.

The chairs have caning on their backs, as also have the table-ends. The chair backs are set at a slight angle not absolutely vertical, as is nearly every other example of Wright's tall-backed dining chairs.

ALINE BARNSDALL (HOLLYHOCK) HOUSE, LOS ANGELES, CALIFORNIA, 1920 DINING ROOM

Room sizes are usually in proportion to the overall size of the building, and larger houses are assumed to have more people living in them. The Hollyhock House does not mirror this generality. The small table has a hexagonal top and a dining chair for each of the six sides.

One side of the room has a wall of doors that open into the courtyard, opposite which are the windows shown in this photograph.

This is one of the few dining rooms before the Usonian era that had fully wood-cladded walls. Between the boards are strips of beaded trim with hexagons to match the table top. Most of Wright's dining tables had at least four legs. This table has a single pedestal.

The chairs are the first radical departure from the ubiquitous tall-backed spindle chairs, often called spinal-column chairs because of the three dimensional carvings on their backs. The insides of their backs had fabric pads attached through small holes near the tops.

It is not known if there were any custom carpets made for this room.

the result of his interest in the Orient. Chinese and Japanese two-dimensional art is simply and directly presented. There are objects in the foreground, middle-ground and background, with simple scenes that make these planes more obvious and distinct. This three-part division in two dimensions was also reflected in Wright's drawings of both exteriors and interiors and is in parallel with Oriental methods.

Wright's interiors mirrored these concepts by providing a sense of high and low, near and far. The decks that Wright threw across his spaces to define each function or room were the elements that allowed him to execute these ideas. It has been noted by many authors that upon entering many of Wright's

major rooms, the space appears squeezed before it is allowed to explode into the actual room. This compression was accomplished by drawing the walls of the entrance in close and dropping the ceiling to just above the height of the client, which has the effect of making the main room seem larger by comparison. A 10-ft (3-m) ceiling would seem all the higher when the entry ceiling was pitched at only 6ft (2m), and would make the higher ceiling appear to be more than double this size.

The near and far were defined by the changes of ceiling level as well as by the bays and inglenooks to be found in many of Wright's designs. Wright's interiors are far more complex than those prevalent at the time and all too common

IMPERIAL HOTEL, TOKYO, JAPAN, 1914–1922
RECONSTRUCTION, BELOW
A small section of the original building was reconstructed at the Meiji Mura open-air museum near Nagoya. This part spanned the two major wings that held the guest rooms.

LOBBY RECONSTRUCTION (OPPOSITE)
This is what greeted visitors as they entered the hotel. As in some of Wright's residential designs, he managed to create surprise and excitement as one entered a grand space. This was achieved by first passing through a low-ceilinged area which suddenly gave way to a three-storied space, lit brilliantly from above.

JOHN STORER HOUSE, LOS ANGELES, CALIFORNIA, 1923

None of the furniture assembled below is original to the Storer House, and as there are no known photographs of the interior of the house when the Storers lived there, it is not known if any was especially designed for it.

The couch and chair in the background were actually designed for the nearby Hollyhock House of a few years earlier, while the tall-backed dining chair is from the Exhibition House that was once on the site of the Guggenheim Museum in New York. The small triangular table is one of a series of production designs by Heritage-Henredon.

This room is on the upper level of the house and has windows to both north and south. The view from the south-facing windows is a wonderful one across the Los Angeles basin, and on clear days, all the way to the Pacific Ocean.

today – simple box-like affairs with flat walls, square corners, and holes for windows and doors.

Wright was able to see his interiors in his mind's eye, even before he put pencil to paper to communicate his ideas to his employees, apprentices, clients and contractors. It has always been difficult to reconcile three-dimensional spaces to two-dimensional drawings, but this did not seem to apply in Wright's case.

Fortunately, it is now possible to examine the buildings, Wright's drawings in hand; but to attempt to

EDGAR J. KAUFMANN HOUSE (FALLINGWATER), MILL RUN, PENNSYLVANIA, 1936

Wright's designs were always extraordinarily skilful and ingenious, but, at Fallingwater, his powers seemed to have reached their apogee. It is immediately apparent that as much care was given to the interior as the exterior, and it is now regarded as a landmark of modern architecture and a work of genius.

The cantilevers extend the living room, integrating it with the waterfall and the surrounding landscape in a particularly romantic way. Beneath this romanticism, however, lies a firm grasp of modern technology which enabled Wright to create a daring and modern concept.

understand them without seeing them in three dimensions is rather more difficult. It is therefore doubtful if many of Wright's clients truly understood what was in store for them. They had faith in Wright's ability to sell them an idea, which they accepted in good faith, and which Wright was certainly qualified to deliver.

The ingenuity of Wright's designs can be perceived in his plans of the buildings. This is not to say that they can be comprehended at once, but the complexity and the unusual nature of the designs is more than obvious. However, this level of expertise usually made for a more expensive construction. While a

simple Thoreau box is the cheapest to build, a Wright house may be the most expensive.

Wright was able, through all the experience he had gained, to determine costs in advance and he did try to make economies where he could. However, at the end of the day, did Wright deliver what he promised? The answer is a resounding affirmative: the fact that there is such intense interest in his work to this day, points to their uniqueness. Did the original clients fully appreciate them? Again yes. As a group, they were Wright's most enthusiastic supporters; they admired his work, and begrudged him not one of their hard-earned dollars.

EDGAR J. KAUFMANN HOUSE (FALLINGWATER), MILL RUN, PENNSYLVANIA, 1936 LIVING ROOM (LEFT AND OVERLEAF)

In these photographs, the arrangement of the original Kaufmann furniture is in accordance with Wright's original plan. The cantilevers and interdigitations of the building are paralled, but on a smaller scale, while the functional is retained, providing a space where the family could gather together.

BEDROOM (BELOW)

Wright understood the rather damp microclimate created by the little valley and provided designs that would allow for air movement within the built-in storage cabinets; in fact, there are pull-out shelves with caning set into them to allow the air to circulate. The American walnut veneer used throughout the house is used in the cabinets as well as on the bed's headboard and there is a useful swivel lamp to illuminate the bed.

The framed Japanese print that hangs above the bed is one of several that Wright gave to the Kaufmanns to place in various locations throughout the house and guest house.

When viewing a Wright interior, try to imagine it with one or more of the elements described above missing. Imagine it without the trim or with flat ceilings or with single windows replacing banks of casements. You will then realize that their character is dramatically changed, and this is what happens when Wright's original interiors are

JOHNSON WAX ADMINISTRATION BUILDING, RACINE, WISCONSIN, 1936
This photograph, taken from Herbert Johnson's helicopter, clearly shows the overall plan as Wright conceived it. The original building ended just to the left of the Research Tower which was added around 1944. The upper-level executive offices and the ventilation nostrils can be seen towards the centre of the administrative office block.

LOBBY (OPPOSITE)
As with the Imperial Hotel (page 49), the entry of the Johnson Wax building has the same sequence of spaces graduating from the outside to the tall lobby within.

altered. When the trim is painted out, it is no longer what Wright envisaged; his creation is diminished. Less serious is when Wright's original colours are changed to what subsequent owners, who are no longer in tune with Wright's original perception of their house, feel are now more fashionable.

During the Prairie era and up to the 1930s, the trim was certainly one of the most important features of the interior. It led the eye from one element to the other, becoming a means of organizing the overall space. It added definition in a most dramatic way. It became the borders and the edges of each

plane. It framed the colour of each panel of each wall, as well as each window and door, making them more important as a result.

Wright used this device to enhance that which it surrounds, in the way an elegant frame enhances a work of art. In a Wright building, however, the interior itself is the work of art. This may be why Wright did not approve of extraneous pictures on his walls; he considered that he was creating all the art that was necessary.

The trim also added to the three-dimensional quality of each wall panel. It altered scale and changed perspective. It also provided a strong visual accent

when its darker, walnut-mahogany colour was contrasted with pea-soup green or a golden-rod ochre walls.

When walking in the countryside, wherever one looks there is something to delight the eye; there is an oak tree or maybe a snow-capped mountain in the distance; a Guernsey cow, or a field of sunflowers, as well as broad areas of grass and sky; there are smaller things to look at, such as a flower or a distant bird. In terms of a building, Wright provides such parallels. Its overall form, and its position in the landscape, may well represent the mountain, and the walls a field of flowers, their petals repeated in the patterns of the art-glass windows. On taking a closer look, one might begin to appreciate the texture of the plaster as well as the grain of the quarter-sawn oak.

The form of the windows, and their location, is never a matter of chance; they are there for a purpose. Wright was not only framing a pleasant view, he was presenting a new way of seeing the world while allowing light to enter.

During the Prairie era, full banks of casement windows were designed to give a wide, panoramic view not possible with the single, double-hung windows of the time, which brought the flow of life and landscape vividly to life within the confines of a building.

**HERBERT E. JOHNSON HOUSE
(WINGSPREAD), WIND POINT, RACINE,
WISCONSIN, 1937**

*After the Johnson Wax Building,
Frank Lloyd Wright followed it up
with a house for its proprietor,
Herbert Johnson. This dramatic
room is at the centre of the house,
surmounted by a clerestoried dome
and focused on the central mass of
a brick fireplace. This is one of five
distinct areas, sometimes called the
upper living room, which is up a
flight of stairs and above the
library.*

TALIESIN WEST, SCOTTSDALE, ARIZONA, 1938

Every autumn, when the Fellowship returned to camp, as Wright's apprentices referred to Taliesin West, there was always more work to be done, in a continuous expansion and improvement of the building.

In the earliest days, the task had been to erect structures that would protect them from the weather, the canvas roof of the drafting room being the first to go up each year.

After the core buildings had been completed and improved, others serving an even greater number of functions were designed, which the apprentices built with their own hands.

Wright understood the desert climate and was able to solve the problems it presented. The theatre, right, is a good example. Grade or ground level corresponds with the bases of he windows, while the entry consists of a set of stairs leading down to where the screen is, and next to a Steinway grand piano. At least half of the room is below grade, taking advantage of the much cooler below-surface temperatures. The roof and ceiling are constructed of concrete and are also designed to keep the room cool.

The tables and chairs could be arranged to accommodate different types of functions. They could be for meals, as shown, such as the formal Taliesin Saturday night dinners, or the tables collapsed and the chairs turned to the front for live performances or movies.

The small Italian Christmas tree lights on the ceiling give an added sparkle to the room after dark.

59

TALIESIN WEST, SCOTTSDALE, ARIZONA, 1938 LIVING ROOM

For the most part, this was the Wrights' personal living room, but after Wright died, his wife used the room to serve cocktails before adjourning to another part of the campus for the formal Saturday night dinner.

This is a large room and set at 90 degrees to the similarly constructed drafting room, which is on the other side of the kitchen.

Light came into the room during the day by means of translucent roof panels, which replaced the canvas structure used in the first years of Taliesin West.

As in many of Wright's houses, there is built-in seating along the side of the room which, because of its size, can accommodate many people either seated or standing.

The furniture is an eclectic mix of original Wright designs, some covered with sheepskins, while others came from local stores.

Wright was famous for his furniture, which he designed especially for particular interiors when nothing else would do. He was interested in his clients and the kinds of lives they lived. His aim was to make life as comfortable as possible for them, so everything is where it is supposed to be. There is light where one might wish to read, and a fireplace at the centre of the house as a potent symbol of hearth and home.

Bedrooms had good closets, dining rooms had storage for linens used at table, and there were bookcases and cabinets for

POPE-LEIGHY HOUSE, WOODLAWN, VIRGINIA, 1940 LIVING ROOM

The Pope-Leighy House was designed on a small budget, but nevertheless has a small but workable living room complete with custom furniture. The line of individual chairs to the left of the photograph are not attached to the wall and are designed to replace the usual built-in banquettes often seen in other Wright-designed houses. This also makes for more versatility, as the chairs can be arranged in various configurations throughout the house. Pope was a journalist and wrote an article praising his house, which did Wright no harm at all.

JOHN C. PEW HOUSE, SHOREWOOD HILLS, MADISON, WISCONSIN, 1940

LIVING ROOM

As in the Tomek and Robie Houses of over 30 years earlier, the ceilings have more than one height, which may not be as apparent in this house because the entire ceiling is covered in beautiful wide boards, lapped and mitred at the corners.

The stone used throughout the house and shown here in the fireplace is very similar to that used at Taliesin and the Unitarian Meeting House nearby in Madison. The block lintel above the firebox makes a dramatic feature in an already powerful structure. The tables and some of the chairs were custom-designed for the Pews.

SOLOMON R. GUGGENHEIM MUSEUM, NEW YORK, 1943–1959

The visitors' entry is at street level without the need to climb a flight of stairs, unlike other more formal art museums, some of which are located along Fifth Avenue. Here at the Guggenheim, the entrance is covered and protected from the elements, and is situated at the centre of the long façade as one proceeds in through the door.

INTERIOR RAMPS (OPPOSITE ABOVE)
Wright's astonishing idea was to

take an elevator to the top of his building, then take a gentle stroll along the descending spiral ramp while enjoying the art.

Not surprisingly, there were critics who questioned the suitability of such a structure as a place to display great art. In fact, some would feel that the building itself offers too much competition and is a distracting influence. But it is magnificent for all that.

THE CUPOLA (OPPOSITE BELOW)
The structural support that holds the

translucent panels of the cupola in place is as fine a work of art as one would expect to see in any Wright building on any scale. It is the main illumination by day, with artificial light installed along the spiral ramp.

Initially, the design was based on circles in much the same style as the low dome at the Johnson Wax building of 20 years earlier. These circles were interlocked and provided a very dramatic arrangement, as does the stirrup design used here.

displaying personal objects at locations around the house.

For the most part, floors are on a single level throughout the house, which makes for easy movement from place to place. Even on a steeply sloped site, such as Fallingwater, every floor is on a single level. However, the ceilings are quite another story, and it is here that most of the complexity of the spaces is expressed. Even in Fallingwater's simple interior, attention is focused on the ceiling, enhancing the space leading to the famous waterfall outside.

By such means is form given to space. Many examples of cathedral or pitched ceilings exist in Wright houses, where he used various structural devices to accommodate changes in form and height.

65

KENNETH LAURENT HOUSE, ROCKFORD, ILLINOIS, 1949 BELOW
Just inside the entrance is this living room area with its fireplace and bench seating adjacent to it. In the background is the dining area separated by Wright's distinctive pole lamp by the brick wall.

HERMAN T. MOSSBERG HOUSE, SOUTH BEND, INDIANA 1949 BELOW RIGHT
The high cathedral ceiling of the living room is one of the most imposing of the late Usonian era. Wright had used strips of wood trim on his ceilings for most of his career and for the most part they mirror the roof's insulated rafters. Jack Howe, Wright's draftsman, had a hand in the design.

RAYMOND CARLSON HOUSE, PHOENIX, ARIZONA, 1950

The intention behind the design of the Carlson house was economy, as with many other projects of this and other periods of Wright's career.

The interior of the Carlson House is as spatially complex as its exterior. The house is based on a module of 2ft (5cm) from centreline to centreline. The 4 x 4-in (10 x 10-cm) wooden framework is centred on the 2-ft marks which makes the distance between the members less than 2ft.

The scale of the house appears larger because of the unfamiliarity of buildings on a 2-ft grid. In the far wall, the wooden members are on a 4-ft centre.

The area below the two hassocks in the picture on the right is the dining room, while stairs to the left lead up to a bathroom and two bedrooms. The fireplace is constructed from simple concrete bricks that continue to form a long bench seat.

Wright also designed custom furniture for Carlson, who was the editor of Arizona Highways *and an enthusiastic promoter of Wright's work.*

ROBERT L. WRIGHT HOUSE, BETHESDA, MARYLAND, 1953

Robert Llewellyn Wright was the youngest of Wright's four sons, born in Oak Park in 1903. He was an attorney in the Washington, DC area for many years and was the second son to ask his father to design a house for him, the first being David, whose house was built in Phoenix just a few years earlier. The two eldest sons were both architects who at certain times in their lives worked for their father.

David Wright's house is based on a circular theme, as is this one for Robert. There is only one complete circle and it accommodates the kitchen and stairway to the second floor. The plan of the house is much like an American football, with curved sides that come to a point at each end.

After passing through a low entrance, one comes into this tall living room with its south-facing windows and glass doors. The floor is concrete and the heating pipes below give an even heat to the room. Much of the furniture is custom-designed and mirrors the plan of the house in the coffee table with hassocks on four sides of it.

The table lamp on the left side, on the counter, is a recent reproduction produced by the author's company, Heinz & Co.

The Davidson House of Buffalo utilizes a simple cantilevered truss involving the roof overhang and soffit to support the roof rafter on its way to the ridge. The Coonley House has a steel frame with connections to support the red tile roof. The corners of the steel frame are not located at the corners of the room. The forward vertical points are within the second window mullion. What would otherwise be an overhang is, in this case, an extension out to the edge of the room. It makes for the smallest corner possible and allows ample

JOHN E. CHRISTIAN HOUSE, WEST LAFAYETTE, INDIANA, 1954

LIVING ROOM (RIGHT ABOVE AND BELOW)
The split-level living room works most successfully in the Christian House. It allows for several viewpoints within the room, as well as accommodating a large number of guests in perfect comfort.

All of the furniture was custom-designed by Wright for this house, including the first TV tables that could be easily dismantled and stored when not in use.

This is one of the finest of Frank Lloyd Wright's Usonian houses, and it has been placed in trust to ensure its future survival.

DINING ROOM (LEFT)

BETH SHOLOM SYNAGOGUE, ELKINS PARK, PHILADELPHIA, PENNSYLVANIA, 1954

The interior of this assembly in many ways resembles the drafting room at Taliesin West in that it is a combination of structure and translucent panels. Overlapping fibreglass sheets allow glare-free light to flood the interior, and even in full sunlight, it is not overpowering. At night it is a different story when the surrounding area is flooded with the light emanating from the building.

Inside, the floor is sloped and gives each member of the congregation an unobstructed view of the proceedings from every angle.

In spite of its large volume, the acoustics are superb with only a hint of reverberation.

light to filter into the interior.

The Willitts House also has a steel frame holding the structure in place. It rises next to the high windows along the side walls and up into the attic above the second-floor bedroom, connecting to a truss in the roof. The truss is pierced by two metal rods that are located within the inside corners of the front bedroom balconies and connected at the bottom to steel beams that cross the living room ceiling between the columns. This steel frame is expressed on the exterior and the interior, but its importance is not obvious as the assembly bolts are hidden behind the living room bookcases. In fact, many of Wright's devices seem merely decorative until one understands the importance of the structures within.

CONCLUSION

Wright introduced many visual and structural elements to achieve the tremendous variations seen in his interiors, which he regarded as more important than the exteriors. He seldom discussed his methods, which makes the study and analysis of his work more difficult but all the more rewarding, once they are fully understood.

The principles on which Wright based his life's work allowed him great versatility, as evidenced by the number and variety of buildings that he produced during his long and tempestuous career.

If one were to choose two examples of his buildings, and compare one with the another, one might conclude that they could not be from the hand of the same architect. However, as with most great work, certain characteristics exist which makes them instantly recognizable as the work of one particular artist of genius. Wright

GERALD B. TONKENS HOUSE, AMBERELY VILLAGE, CINCINNATI, OHIO, 1955

The houses that were built using the Usonian Automatic System, a concrete block system invented by Wright, often appear small; but the interior of the Tonkens House is surprisingly large and open between the living and dining areas. The warm wood tones contrast well with the cooler concrete blocks.

had his imitators, which he found irksome: he would have much preferred that his work was fully understood so that it could be a creative impetus to other aspiring architects and designers. Wright held true to his principles all his life and his work reflects the honesty and singlemindedness with which he approached each new project.

THE DALLAS THEATER CENTER (THE KALITA HUMPHREYS THEATER), DALLAS, TEXAS (1955)

The auditorium of the theatre is lit by a row of clerestory windows inserted just below the roof of the main building. The windows are much the same as those used in the Pope-Leighy House (page 62), with a cut-out design that throws ever-changing patterns of light into the interior as the day progresses.

At night, the friendly glow of the interior welcomes guests as they arrive for a performance. The main entrance is to the left of the top photograph.

ANNUNCIATION GREEK ORTHODOX CHURCH, WAUWATOSA, MILWAUKEE, WISCONSIN, 1956

Both Beth Sholom Synagogue and the Annunciation Church work well in their individual ways, even though they were designed with very different religious philosophies in mind.

Instead of a tall translucent roof, however, the congregation of Annunciation was given a beautiful dome that appears to hang suspended above a continuous row of pearl windows set at its base. The dome is fitted with what amounts to ball-bearings, that move as the dome flexes with fluctuating temperatures, which prevents the concrete of the dome from cracking.

The interior carries a suggestion of a Byzantine iconostasis and has the required atmosphere conducive to prayer.

INDEX

Page numbers in italics refer to illustrations